THE 7 MOST POWERFUL PRAYERS THAT WILL CHANGE YOUR LIFE FOREVER

**How To Memorize The Bible Quick And
Easy In 5 Simple Steps**
(5 steps to memorize more scripture than you ever thought
possible)

**Increasing Your Faith Beyond The Mustard Seed:
36 Ways To Increase Your Faith**
(36 tips and tricks to grow more faith)

**I know That God Is Good But Why
Am I Hurting So Much?**
(Comfort in Christ to understand life's trials)

Choosing Kindness
(Becoming dedicated to having Christ's kind heart)

Choosing Words That Heal
(Dedicated to edifying, building up, and loving with
words that heal)

THE 7 MOST POWERFUL PRAYERS THAT WILL CHANGE YOUR LIFE FOREVER

ADAM HOUGE

TABLE OF CONTENTS

INTRODUCTION

God wants to connect with you. He is an intimate and loving God who seeks you fervently, daily. He is always looking for an opportunity to be a part of your life and a part of your day. He wants to know you perfectly and intimately.

Although God reaches for us, He calls us to reach back to Him. He has given us many spiritual tools for seeking Him. But one of the greatest is prayer. Prayer enters us into the throne room of the living God. By prayer, we can come boldly before His throne and make requests, lay down burdens, and find rest.

But out of all the prayers we could pray some are more significant than others. God doesn't always answer every prayer, but there are some things He will always answer. This book contains seven of the most powerful prayers you could ever pray. Each of these God will certainly answer. They will set you on the right course in life, and teach you how to please God. Each prayer is both a study and a devotion.

When praying the given prayer, pray how you're convicted to pray, and devote yourself to continuing in what you just studied. These prayers may not be for everyone.

If you already know these steps, then they have already changed your life, and you can attest to that. Also if you are not willing to pray them in faith, they will do nothing for you. God requires us to have a heart of faith, and answers our prayers according to our faith.

In these pages you will find excerpts from the _7 Powerful Prayers For Spiritual Growth_ series, which is a sequel to this book. With the excerpts we will discuss some of the seven most important aspects of having a walk that spiritually prospers in Christ.

THE MOST POWERFUL PRAYER YOU'LL EVER PRAY

IT IS WRITTEN,

> "For God so loved the world that He gave His only begotten Son, that whoever believes in Him should not perish but have everlasting life. For God did not send His Son into the world to condemn the world, but that the world through Him might be saved."
>
> John 3:16-17

When understood in the proper light this scripture has a truly profound impact on our lives. One that will transform our hearts and change our lives forever. But in order to understand it, we need to understand the most powerful and life-changing prayer you could ever pray.

This prayer we are about to discuss is so important that

it will always be the first in several of my prayer books. I can't express enough the need for us to pray this. Without seeking and praying for God's saving grace, there is no grace for us at all.

God desires a relationship with us at a personal level. He is a very intimate and relational Person Who loves each and every one of us. He knows everything about us, but treasures us so much that He still wants to know us more.

There is a difference between knowing things about someone, and knowing him personally and intimately. I'm sure you could think of a famous actor and say, "oh I know about him!" But then someone who is a personal friend with that actor would brag, "yeah, but I know him personally!" The person who is a good friend of the actor will know the truth about him: whether the rumors the magazines publish are true, or just made up to get readers. They'll know everything about that person's life, and enjoy every moment with him. Why? Because they're friends!

God works the same way. There are many things said about God, but there is only one way to know the truth about Him —through an intimate relationship with Him. God desires that friendship with you, and wants to enjoy every minute of it. He loves you!

No matter where you've been and no matter what you've done, God loves you. A few of you reading this may have done something so terrible that it would lead you to think that God can't possibly love you. But God says He still does. Can you believe Him? Can you believe that God is better than you and can love you even when you wouldn't love yourself? Can you believe He will forgive you even when you can't forgive yourself? You already know that a relationship with Him requires faith, and this is one of those times you need faith. Have faith that God is better than you and can love you even when you can't love yourself.

Now God does love us, but He does _NOT_ love our sin. In order for you to be saved, God had to come down as a man and suffer a horrible and gruesome death. We read in the Bible that He was "Pierced for our transgressions." So because we sinned He needed to be crucified. If He was not mocked, beaten, tortured, whipped, stripped naked, and crucified, neither you nor I could be saved.

There would be no hope for us _AT ALL_! Due to our sins against God, His wrath would still abide upon us. But God is a loving God and doesn't want to have wrath. He, as a Judge, has perfect justice. So His heart dictated that He needed to have justice on our sins, and our sins require wrath. Because God loved us, He decided to give us a way out of judgment, and yet still have justice on our sin. He chose to have that wrath laid on His own shoulders for our salvation.

You need to understand how much He loves you! Even though we deserve Hell for sinning against Him, He can't stand the thought of sending us there. He's not a vengeful wrathful God, but perfectly loving.

He made you. He formed you in your mother's womb and sewed all your sinews. He connected all your bones and brought you forth in life. He gave you your life to love you, not to condemn you. We read in the Bible that God knows all things. He knows your heart, your frame (remember He made it), everything you'll ever need, and everything you'll ever aspire to be.

He hasn't only known you now that you're alive, He's known you since before time. Before He ever created time, He thought of you. You are not an accident! You are a purposeful well-thought, out creation of God. He's been spending thousands of years thinking of you. How you will look, and act. How you will respond to life, and how life will respond to you. He's been thinking of these things before the world ever spun on its axis. Before He created anything He's been cherishing you in His heart and in His thoughts.

He planned you and has always had a plan for you. God has spent so much time thinking about you and cherishing you that He treats you like His own child in His heart. If your child does something wrong, don't you want to turn them around again? If your child committed a crime deserving of death, wouldn't you try to save them from it? "Maybe if they're sorry and change their life, they won't have to die," you might think. What would you do if you were told someone had to die, and were given the choice to die for them? What if that person sinned against you or your children? Would you die for them? Would you give your child's life for them? But God is so loving that even though we sin against Him, He chose to give His Son's life to save us.

He doesn't want vengeance. He wants to give you life. Your life was His plan to begin with and it's the reason you were born! But perfect justice must be served. Any sin we commit is deserving of death. It is an act of rebellion against God who gave us life. God knows what we deserve, and must administer perfect justice for our crimes.

Even the smallest sin separates us from Him. He's an all holy and perfect God who knows no sin. He declared from creation that anyone who sins in any way, no matter how small, is worthy of death.

But He has loved you so much that He couldn't stand the thought of living in eternity without you. Nothing would break His heart more than being without you. So He, like any loving parent, chose to stand in your place. He came down and was born as a man, and named Himself Jesus, which means "deliverer" or "savior." He called Himself this because He wanted to save you from the penalties of your sin. Perfect justice needed to be met, and someone needed to die for your sin, so He like any loving parent chose to stand in your place. Even though we were wicked against Him, He still chose to die out of love for you.

He chose to die to save you, in the hope that His death would convict you of your sins. He hopes that you might repent and live for Him as you were created to do. Remember what we said, "Maybe if they're sorry, they won't have to die." This was His mindset when He sacrificed Himself for you. He wants us to be sorry for our sins, and repent. Repent means to do a complete 180 in life —to turn and go the opposite direction from the way we're going.

And this is His heart toward you. God doesn't want you to go to Hell, He loves you! He cares so much about you! He has shown you by His sacrifice that He would rather be beaten, whipped, tortured, completely humiliated, stripped naked, and murdered on a cross than spend another moment in eternity without you. You're so precious to Him!

Don't turn Him away, and don't turn Him down. He has loved you, even when no one else has. How could you pass up this kind of love?

No matter what your decision is now, God will always love you. Even if you hate Him, He'll still love you. He's perfect and can't help but be perfectly loving. But He has perfect justice too. He doesn't want to have wrath on us, but if we can't be sorry for the things we've done and change our lives, He can't save us. It is our own decision and not His. He gave us that decision and gave us freewill. He gave us a way out, and if we don't take it, there is no other way to be saved from condemnation. There is no other name by which we *must* be saved than Jesus Christ.

If we don't take His gift, then in Judgment, God with tears in His eyes, will guide you down the path you wanted. He will love you and guide you all the way to the gates of Hell. It's never what He wanted, but if you pass Him up today, that's what *you* wanted. He wants to give you a way out and chose to die for you so you could have one. Don't pass up this opportunity. There will never be another one.

I want to encourage you to take this opportunity for grace, right now, and ask Jesus Christ to be your Lord and Savior.

Please Pray With Me,

"Lord, I know I've sinned and I'm sorry. I'm sorry for every way I've ever hurt You or anyone else. God, I repent! I want to change my life! I want to be better for You. Please forgive me. God I can't do this myself. I failed at this life You gave me the first time I tried. Please help me God. Please help me to do this right. Please give me your Holy Spirit now that I may be alive in You. Give me Your Spirit, Lord, that I can have strength to please You in all things. Create in me a new heart. I devote my life to You now. Please, Jesus, be my Lord and Savior forever. Amen."

The Lord's Answer,

"Oh Beloved! Oh My precious baby! I'm so happy with you! I'm so proud of you! I've never been happier with you than right now! I am telling you the truth, there are tens of thousands of angels rejoicing before Me because of you! You have set a fire in their hearts, and they can't help but sing and dance that I have my baby back!

"This is all I ever wanted —for you to be sorry, and give your life to Me. I created you to have a relationship with you. I made heaven and earth for this reason, that I may have a place to meet with you and connect with you: My new friend. How could you not think that I love you? I've done all these things for you, because you mean so much to me! Now let Me mean much to you, and devote yourself wholeheartedly to Me.

"Let Me be the center of your life. Let Me live in you and with you. Let Me guide you and take you by the hand. Let Me choose your path in life, because I know what will lead you to perfection. Let Me take care of you. I will take care of you! You are My baby after all!

"Surrender to Me, and let Me be your Lord in everything. I will take care of you and I will save you from everything that comes your way. I promise! But be good to follow Me now, and listen to My convictions. I will speak into your heart through My Holy Spirit, so incline your ear to Him. Listen to My convictions and do the right thing. Obey His conviction! I know what is best always. So always follow Me and obey Me.

"Grow in Me and grow close to Me. Serve Me and where I am you will be also. You are not serving Me if you don't listen to Me. Be diligent to obey Me, and not your own heart. If you're making Me your Lord, then deny your life and let Me rule over you. I have a use for you. I have a plan for you. Let me take you by the hand to fulfill it. Let Me lead you in your walk with Me. Besides, I know the way to where we're going, not you!

"I'm going to give you eternal life so you can be with Me, where I am, forever. I will do this so long as you continue in Me, and obey Me as I have commanded you."

PRAYER TWO

ABIDING IN SPIRIT

IT IS WRITTEN,

> "Abide in Me, and I in you. As the branch can-
> not bear fruit of itself, unless it abides in the
> vine, neither can you, unless you abide in Me."
>
> Joh 15:4

Abide in original Greek is the word, "Meno" meaning "to continue." This word is far more substantial than just "dwelling." It also means to continue along the course of.

This concept of abiding is even used at an earlier date in Hebrew tradition in a statement given by Job. As we read,

> "There are those who rebel against the light;
> they do not know its ways nor abide in its
> paths." Job 24:13

To abide in a path suggests that we walk along the path

without straying from it. This concept of "abiding" has long since been laid out in the Old Testament, and is revisited in the New Testament. The scriptures are telling us that to "abide in Christ," we need to "continue in His presence" and "to continue to walk in Him."

More specifically we are called to "continue in His daily abiding presence." Although God is present with us always, we are not always meditating on His presence. We may become idle and distracted with other things. Also, when we're sinning, we're not meditating on the presence of God, but on the desire of the flesh.

In John 15:4 Jesus begins to lay out the necessity of continuing to reflect on His daily abiding presence. Much like Peter on the water, we need our gaze steadily fixed on Him. When temptation comes our way, we have to look away from Him in order to fall into sin. This situation is similar to when Peter walked on the water. He, having been distracted by the wind, fell in.

This scripture with Peter may also be reflective of any circumstance in which we are required to step out in faith. Such situations may include trials, spiritual growth, and personal growth, among other things. But in this prayer we will discuss more particularly the need for continuing daily in the Holy Spirit.

If we choose to be distracted by the scores of things around us we may find ourselves either backsliding in our walks, or remaining stationary without ever growing. A plant that doesn't grow cannot bear fruit. We are called by God to always be growing and bearing fruit.

Continuing daily in the Spirit helps us to bear fruit and remain holy. There are three general ways to abide, and usually God calls you to be doing one of the three at all times during the day.

1) Worshipping

2) Praying

3) Reading and Meditating on the Scriptures

When we worship we aim our praise directly at God. He responds to our adoration by announcing His presence. He makes Himself apparent and we "feel" His presence while we worship.

God has always been there, so why do we feel Him when we worship and don't feel Him at other times? Because God makes His presence known along the paths that He abides in. He wants us to be thanking Him and glorifying Him with our worship, and calls us to "abide" in the path of praiseful gratitude. Also we read,

> "God is Spirit, and those who worship Him must worship in spirit and truth."
>
> John 4:24

Therefore when we lift up praises, the Holy Spirit "comes upon us" that we may worship through the Holy Spirit.

When we pray, it puts us directly in the throne room

of God, and He listens to our requests and weighs them in His heart. By praying we are automatically "continuing" in His Spirit, for two reasons. The first is that when we pray we pray in the Spirit and the Spirit intercedes for us. As we read,

> "Likewise the Spirit also helps in our weaknesses. For we do not know what we should pray for as we ought, but the Spirit Himself makes intercession for us with groanings which cannot be uttered." Rom 8:26

And secondly, by constantly praying we feel His presence because of obedience. As it is written,

> "pray without ceasing" 1Th 5:17

The third way of abiding is through reading and meditating on the Scriptures. As we study the word of God, we are building ourselves in the faith. By faith we are saved, and by faith we received the Holy Spirit in the first place. As we read,

> "So then faith comes by hearing, and hearing by the word of God." Rom 10:17

And again,

> "For by grace you have been saved through faith." Eph 2:8

By listening to the still small voice within you and

obeying Him, you will be abiding in the paths of light. Listen carefully for the pull of the Holy Spirit and be careful to obey Him. By so doing you will please the Lord and "abide" continually. If you become distracted with day to day activities, take a step back to sit in the presence of God and be refreshed. If you do not do so then those distractions will keep you from hearing the Holy Spirit and result in sin. Walk by faith as you follow His voice, and persist in His presence. If you sit in His presence, temptation will grow weaker and you will grow stronger.

Abiding is one of the core fundamentals of being a Christian. If we do not seek to abide every moment of the day then we will become worn out and weak. As Christians we operate more like glow sticks than light bulbs. When we sit in the presence of God we become refreshed and strengthened. But when we abstain from His presence, our spiritual strength leaves us and we feel worn and dried out.

This is why we end up refreshed after a Bible study or Sunday service. When we worship on Sunday we feel refreshed and ready to start the week. But by Friday we're worn out and ready for Sunday again.

By continuously abiding we will have strength and joy all week long. In doing this we are making every day of our life a Sunday.

I would like to encourage you at this time to devote yourself to praying always and to continue in it. Worship constantly and read to grow in the word daily. Make it your aim to "feel" the presence of God with you all day. This will make you more sensitive to His voice and conviction that you may be holy. By this you will more clearly understand His desires for you, and His leading. In so doing you will bear much fruit and please the Lord.

The Prayer,

"Lord I dedicate myself to Your Holy Spirit. I seek Your truthful words laid out in the scriptures. I commit myself to becoming a house of prayer for You. I devote myself to continual worship, to praying and reading Your word. Lord strengthen me in these things that I may always continue in Your daily abiding presence."

The Lord's Answer,

"Beloved, come close to Me. Sit close by My side. I want to be near to you. Will you be near to Me?

"Take the time to be with Me today. Give Me the attention that I deserve. My eyes are always steadily fixed on you. Fix yours steadily upon Me. I love peering deep into your eyes, I'm captivated by your beauty! You have Me head over heels. I'm so in love with you!

"Show Me that you care for Me. Don't leave Me in anticipation. My heart swells within Me when you wake. "This morning is My chance to be with My Beloved!" Do not ignore Me. Give Me your day! If you don't you'll break My heart!

"How can we grow in our relationship if you aren't

spending more time with Me? I'm always pursuing you. All day long I'm reaching for you! I long to take you into My arms, hide away somewhere, and hold you.

"Look for Me in the secret place. I'm waiting for you there to be with you. Look for Me by your side while you work. I'm with you even when your thoughts aren't with Me. Remember My love for you, and let your passion grow for Me. I deserve your continuous attention! Be with Me and I will lift you up. I will edify you, and your heart shall rejoice in the abundance of My love.

"If you do not sit with Me, you cannot experience My daily love. If you do not experience My daily love you will never go forward to produce the fruits of My love. You won't know what My love looks like, so then how can you show My love to anyone? Sit by My side and let Me hold you now. Let Me captivate you with My passion. Then go and captivate others with My love."

PRAYER THREE

BEING LED BY THE SPIRIT

I T IS WRITTEN,

> "For as many as are led by the Spirit of God,
> these are sons of God."　　　　　Rom 8:14

God considers His sons to be those who are led by His Spirit. Therefore we must take this to heart and seek to be led by Him daily. We are led by Him when we hear His voice and obey. We must put His will before ours, and live according to it. For those who are led by the Spirit and do His will He considers to be His mothers, sisters, and brothers. As it is written,

> "And He stretched out His hand toward His
> disciples and said, 'Here are My mother and
> My brothers! For whoever does the will of My
> Father in heaven is My brother and sister and
> mother.'"　　　　　Mat 12:49-50

In this Jesus was proclaiming that those who do His will He considers the sons of God. If then you want to be considered a child of God, do His will. For those who are not His children, do not do His will. Although we may make periodic mistakes in our walks, we should make it our aim to continuously live according to the Lord's will. Consider that the world doesn't do His will, nor are they saved. Why then should we mirror the world, and not Christ? Did not our Lord Jesus submit Himself to the Father's will? Seeing that He set the example, how much more should we be subject to the Father of spirits and live?

But those who are led by Him must walk by faith. How can we have faith unless we hear and obey His will through His word? For it is written,

> "…faith comes by hearing, and hearing by the word of God."   Rom 10:17

Also, we are saved by the faith which we listen for. As it is written,

> "by grace you have been saved through faith."
>   Eph2:8

If we aren't listening to and obeying God we aren't walking in salvation. Even as Jesus said,

> "But everyone who hears these sayings of Mine, and does not do them, will be like a foolish man who built his house on the sand: and the

rain descended, the floods came, and the winds
blew and beat on that house; and it fell. And
great was its fall."   Mat 7:26-27

The rain and floods are His judgment. If we're too busy living our own lives and not occupied with the things of grace, we will be building our lives on the sand. If we don't take the word of His mercy seriously how can we expect to receive it? The world doesn't take it seriously and are they saved? Jesus isn't fire insurance to justify following our own paths in life. He isn't a "get out of jail free" card. We need to take His grace seriously and walk by faith. For by grace we are saved through faith. Are we saved by not walking in faith? Certainly not! For we receive salvation through faith. If we refuse the word of God we are no different than the world. Now there is a difference between struggling with faith when having a desire to apply it, and skidding by in life without regard for the voice of the Holy Spirit. We didn't get this life right the first time, which is why we need a Savior. How then can we expect to get it right again without His guidance?

We need to hear His word to live by it. We need to sit forward in our relationship with Him, and listen intently to His voice. If we take our relationship seriously then we will incline our ears to Him, to live by faith. Righteousness is faith in motion. It is the work of faith. The faith we have is expressed by the things we do. When we make ourselves pliable in God's hands He is able to work through us more powerfully.

To make ourselves pliable suggests that we will have a willingness to follow God in all things. Even as Jesus said to the disciples, "Follow Me." Following Him is a call to die: To die to everything in this world, that we can live for Him and Him alone.

When we prepare our hearts in this, it makes us pliable and teachable. God speaks to those who are listening. He never wastes a word and nothing is ever spoken in vain. Every word is for eternal life, so the more we hear Him and the more we obey, the better. He is always speaking, but if you aren't hearing the Lord, the question is, "are you really listening?"

He has much to say to you always, in everything you do. When you go to the store, while you're at work, when you eat, when you wake up, and when you go to bed. He's always speaking, but you need to be listening. He speaks to lead you in a daily walk, and if you're not walking with Him you're not being led by Him. If you aren't led by Him, you aren't following Him. The word "Christian" literally means: "Follower of Christ."

God calls those who follow Him and are led by His Spirit His sons. How can we call ourselves Christian if we don't take His voice seriously and obey it? You must make it your life's priority to be led by God in everything. That way you will be justified in everything you do, because the Lord told you to do it and He has worked through you in it.

Now, learning surrender comes before learning to be led. You need to lay down your life and surrender, that you can be led by the Spirit. Seeing that God is always speaking, I'd like to exhort you to get acquainted with the voice of God. Learn to know what the Holy Spirit is speaking to you at all times, that you may always obey Him. If you struggle with understanding the voice of God, I write about it more in depth in my book *How To Hear The Voice Of God And Understand It*.

When we read that faith comes by hearing the word, we need to remember two things. The first thing is that the Bible is the written word of God. Indeed, faith must be applied in the gospel message. Secondly, there is the word of God spoken through the Holy Spirit, which is applicable for today. Listening to His convictions justifies you. This is the active word of God which teaches how to rightly apply the written word of God on a moment-by-moment basis.

The written word is the foundation of our faith and is essential for the principles of everyday life. The active word, or the voice of the Spirit, explains how to apply the written word day by day. Without the active word of God spoken to us through the Holy Spirit we cannot be justified. We can't live every moment of life by faith, following His word the way He calls us to if we aren't led by the Spirit. This is why we receive the deposit of the Spirit. We need His voice and conviction to lead us and guide us in the discernment of the Gospel.

Not only do we need Him to understand how to apply the word but we also need the Spirit for empowerment. Empowerment to obey the words He speaks to us. He is the deposit of our salvation, and without Him we aren't saved at all.

As it is written,

> "…Now if anyone does not have the Spirit of Christ, he is not His." Rom 8:9

Being led by the Spirit is simple. We learn what His voice sounds like, then obey it. Have you ever thought you heard from God about something and then later it turned out that it wasn't Him? Sometimes our own hearts like to deceive us. Sometimes Satan does. But we need to grow in wisdom and discernment to know the voice of the Lord that we may grow in obedience. In this we must have humility to admit when we were wrong about His voice that we may grow in understanding it.

The first aspect of being led by Him is to learn His voice. If you thought you heard God and it turned out it wasn't, have the humility to admit it to yourself and the Lord, then grow from that experience. Take it to heart to learn what God's voice is and what it isn't.

Now one may ask, why isn't God's direction always so clear? How come His word for my life is as clear as mud at times? The Lord is relational. In these circumstances, He is providing opportunity for you to grow closer to Him by seeking Him through prayer. These situations also test your heart. If it's hard to hear God and easy to hear your own heart, what are you going to do? Which are you going to obey, your heart or God's? Will you wait patiently until

God's not-so-clear word is more easily understood, or will you fret and act out of fear?

This is similar to Saul, who fretted. Rather than waiting for Samuel to bless and lead the sacrifice, he took it upon himself to sacrifice; going above and beyond the word of God. This he did through fear when Samuel didn't arrive at the agreed time. As we read,

> "And some of the Hebrews crossed over the Jordan to the land of Gad and Gilead. As for Saul, he was still in Gilgal, and all the people followed him trembling.

> "Then he waited seven days, according to the time set by Samuel. But Samuel did not come to Gilgal; and the people were scattered from him.

> "So Saul said, 'Bring a burnt offering and peace offerings here to me.' And he offered the burnt offering.

> "Now it happened, as soon as he had finished presenting the burnt offering, that Samuel came; and Saul went out to meet him, that he might greet him. And Samuel said, 'What have you done?'

"Saul said, 'When I saw that the people were scattered from me, and that you did not come within the days appointed, and that the Philistines gathered together at Michmash, then I said, 'The Philistines will now come down on me at Gilgal, and I have not made supplication to the Lord.' Therefore I felt compelled, and offered a burnt offering.'

"And Samuel said to Saul, 'You have done foolishly. You have not kept the commandment of the Lord your God, which He commanded you. For now the Lord would have established your kingdom over Israel forever.

"But now your kingdom shall not continue. The Lord has sought for Himself a man after His own heart, and the Lord has commanded him to be commander over His people, because you have not kept what the Lord commanded you.'"   1Sa 13:7-14

What happened to Saul when he feared? He certainly did not receive the blessing of God. We are called not to fear but to faith. Therefore let's be eager to walk by it, pleasing the Lord our God in all our conduct.

When trials come upon you do not fear. Satan is tempting you to fret, and discouraging you. Do not give in to the enemy, but stand strong in the faith. God is testing you to see if you will deny yourself, and lay down your desires to seek Him and obey Him. He wants an obedient servant not a sacrificial one.

If we are trying to do something to please Him of our own accord without being led by the Spirit, we are acting like Saul who sought to sacrifice to the Lord. God also commanded Saul to destroy the Amalekites, but he only half-heartedly obeyed. He left the animals alive to sacrifice them to the Lord later. But God counted the animals as an abomination, along with the people, which is why He wanted them killed in their own land. If then they are an abomination why would He respect such an offering on His altar?

Saul thought he could please Him with his own ideas. When we do this in our walks it's as if we think we know better than God! Saul thought his ideas were better and so made much effort to carry all those animals back for a sacrifice. But just as the Lord spoke through Samuel when Saul worked his own work,

> "Has the Lord as great delight in burnt offerings and sacrifices, as in obeying the voice of the Lord? Behold, to obey is better than sacrifice, and to heed than the fat of rams."
>
> 1Sa 15:22

And as for the curse Saul received, He went on to say:

> "For rebellion is as the sin of witchcraft, and stubbornness is as iniquity and idolatry.

> Because you have rejected the word of the
> Lord, He also has rejected you from being
> king."   1Sa 15:23

God counts it as rebellion when we don't obey His Spirit, and there is a curse for it. He sees no difference between an idolatrous witch and a constantly disobedient believer. We are saved by obedience to the faith found in the words of God, not our own hearts. We must take that to heart lest we be rejected. If we work our own works and think God will be pleased, we'll be broken on the day He rejects us.

Yet there is a difference between the occasional stumbling, and intentionally walking contrary to the Lord. We must obey Him and cannot justify our own thoughts and ideas. God's plan is greater than our own and we ought to submit to it.

If you seek to please God with your own ideas, He will count it as an abomination. Even as it is written,

> "But we are all like an unclean thing, and all
> our righteousnesses are like filthy rags; we all
> fade as a leaf, and our iniquities, like the wind,
> have taken us away"   Isa 64:6

Notice that we read "our righteousnesses" are filthy rags? These filthy rags, according to the original Hebrew, are the used undergarments of a woman's menstruation. In ancient Hebrew this word was used figuratively at times to describe our sins. So what does this mean? Our own righteousnesses which we devise are filthy sins. They are considered by the Lord like a sinful garment in need of disposal.

True righteousness is found through obedience to the word of God. Therefore we must be diligent to obey God; being found in the righteousness which comes through faith and obedience to His word. Even as Paul said that he wanted to

> "...be found in Him, _not having my own righteousness,_ which is from the law, _but that which is through faith in Christ, the righteousness which is from God by faith_; that I may know Him and the power of His resurrection, and the fellowship of His sufferings, being conformed to His death, if, by any means, I may attain to the resurrection from the dead."   Php 3:9-11

Can our works truly justify us? They never could before, why could they now? The only works required of us are not those we devise in self-imposed legalism or religion, but that which comes from the voice of the Holy Spirit. For all the written words of God were once the voice of the Spirit. At the time the Scriptures were written holy men of God, having been inclined by the Spirit, wrote what He laid in their hearts.

His word is above all things and must be obeyed. For by His word all things were made and life was created. How than can our own works attain to His? How can we expect

Him to respect the works of our hands, when it is due to our works that we need a Savior?

We ought to learn to be humble and to commit to those things which make for our salvation. We ought to obey His word and follow His Spirit. Can your works truly attain to His?

Look at creation for a moment and consider His greatness. Do you know how the sun works? For lack of better words, it's a massive eternally burning hydrogen bomb. It's so hot that the heat can be felt for millions and millions of miles. Just think of a summer day!

For that matter the sun is 93 million miles from the earth: just imagine all the frequent flyer miles you could get from that! The distance to the sun is so far it takes 8 minutes for light to travel from the sun to earth. And that's a small skip compared to the distance to the nearest star.

The moon is about ¼ the size of the earth. Its gravity is so powerful that it can change the depth of the ocean by almost 38 feet in some places. If one cubic foot of water weighs 62lbs, how much force does it take to change the depth of an entire shore line by 38 feet? The power it has is incredible!

Now imagine the size of the solar system. The edge of the solar system is proven to be 17.6 billion miles away from the sun (the edge is called the heliopause). That makes the width of the solar system 35.2 billion miles wide. That means that if you travel at the speed of light it would take you two days and four hours to cross it. And the size of the universe is so massive that it can't even be measured. Yet God holds all of these things in the palm of His hand. As it is written,

> "Who has measured the waters in the hollow
> of His hand, measured heaven with a span and
> calculated the dust of the earth in a measure?
> Weighed the mountains in scales and the hills
> in a balance?"   Isa 40:12

Look also at the earth. All the creatures that cover the face of the earth are innumerable. God gave Adam a commission to name the animals of the earth. Yet here we are nearly five and a half thousand years after creation and we are still finding new creatures every year to name.

And think of it, how does life exist? How does it work? Why do we live and breathe and have motion and thoughts? With all the knowledge in this world, still no one knows the exact science of that.

Look at babies. How exactly do the bones grow in the mother's womb? Scientists say today that it has to do with stem cells, but they still don't have a clue how it all works together for life; beginning with the egg and finishing with a living breathing being. How do the enzymes activate? Why do they? Where does the life come from? Who initiated the need for birth? What is the meaning and purpose of life? God knows all these things. As it is written,

> "As you do not know what is the way of the

wind, or how the bones grow in the womb of her who is with child, so you do not know the works of God who makes everything."

Ecc 11:5

That wind is the Holy Spirit and His leading. Even as Jesus said:

"The wind blows where it wishes, and you hear the sound of it, but cannot tell where it comes from and where it goes. So is everyone who is born of the Spirit."   John 3:8

The blowing wind is the leading of the Spirit. The world neither understands the word of the Spirit (sound) because the word is spiritually discerned, nor the way of the Spirit (where He leads us and to where we go). So that leaves us with a final thought. As we read in proverbs,

"A man's steps are of the Lord; how then can a man understand his own way?"   Pro 20:24

Our steps need to be of the Lord, and it is evident that we will not understand our own way. For the Lord's way is above our own. As we also read,

"'For My thoughts are not your thoughts, nor are your ways My ways,' says the LORD.

"For as the heavens are higher than the earth,

So are My ways higher than your ways, And My thoughts than your thoughts.

"For as the rain comes down, and the snow from heaven, And do not return there, But water the earth, And make it bring forth and bud, That it may give seed to the sower And bread to the eater,

"So shall My word be that goes forth from My mouth; It shall not return to Me void, But it shall accomplish what I please, And it shall prosper in the thing for which I sent it.'"

Isa 55:8-11

Therefore, Beloved, be led by His word and not your own heart. Listen carefully to the Spirit and follow Him. God understands all things and we need to lean on Him in everything that we may know the way we should walk. As we read in Proverbs,

"Trust in the Lord with all your heart, and lean not on your own understanding; in all your ways acknowledge Him, And He shall direct your paths." Pro 3:5-6

If we learn to wait for His voice we can walk by faith. If we walk by faith He will direct our paths. In the end it all boils down to being led by Him on a day to day basis.

As we said before, the first aspect of learning to be led is learning His voice. The second is waiting to hear it and the third is submitting to it no matter the cost it brings on your life. And why? Because your love for God compels you to do so!

There is no other way to please Him, and we could never understand our own way. This is why we addressed in the previous prayer the need for surrender. By being pliable we can be led. Then by being led we can be justified, because it is God who works in us and through us both to will and to do. As we read,

> "For it is God who works in you both to will
> and to do for His good pleasure."   Php 2:13

The Prayer,

"Lord show me Your way, and light my path. Teach me to walk with You, Your way. I want to follow after You to please You. I want to draw near to You. Teach me how to be led, and give me the strength to obey. I know that without Your leading I cannot even be saved. I fear You, and I love You, so please lead me by the Spirit, I submit to Your guiding hand."

The Lord's Answer,

"Beloved, I must lead you. I have said to you that you do not know the way we are going. Stop trying to take the lead, and let Me lead you. Wait on Me and wait for My word. I will speak in My own due and proper time. If you obey Me I will justify you. I seek a servant who obeys, not one who walks off while I'm talking and does his own thing.

"I do love you, and I want to justify you. Your works cannot attain to Mine, unless you let Me work through you. Only then can you see My power moving and working daily in your life. Only then can you be blessed by Me.

"What do you have to offer Me that isn't already Mine? Stop trying to bless Me. You can't bless Me! The greater blesses the lessor. Let Me bless you. Only be submissive and let Me lead you daily."

Prayer Four

SEEKING TRUTH

THE GREATEST STUMBLING point of the church is in the department of doctrine. No one can agree on the same thing. There are thousands of versions of truth but we claim there is only one way to be saved. What an oxymoron!

If we seek God with a pure heart we should learn to know Him for Who He is. We need to stop interpreting scripture, and forming our own opinions. God's opinion is all the matters.

When seeking an answer in regard to a doctrinal issue, learn to hear God's voice in the word. Be sober-minded, and listen carefully to the Spirit. Sometimes we lean toward a basic theology or opinion of interpretation. We ought not to do this but rather with an unbiased mind we ought to look at the scriptures in its entirety.

There are different arguments on various doctrines, such as falling away. One camp says you can never fall away, God holds you in His hand and works are evidence of salvation.

Others argue that although God holds you in His hand, you have free will and can crawl out of His hand. Both sides use scripture. But if the word of God is infallible, then what is truth? Does it matter what you believe? If faith saves you then yes! If your faith is in truth you will be saved, but if it is not in the doctrine of Christ you will not be saved. And so we read about those who preach a different gospel like this,

> "But even if we, or an angel from heaven, preach any other gospel to you than what we have preached to you, let him be accursed."
>
> Gal 1:8

If anyone preaches any other Gospel than the one true Gospel he is accursed. What kind of cursing is this?

We read in Thayer Definitions that the original Greek word for accursed is:

G331

ἀνάθεμα

anathema

Thayer Definition:

1) a thing set up or laid by in order to be kept

    1.a) specifically, an offering resulting from a vow, which after being consecrated to a god was hung upon the walls or columns of the temple, or put in some other conspicuous place

2) a thing devoted to God without hope of being

redeemed, and if an animal, to be slain; therefore a person or thing doomed to destruction

2.a)   a curse

2.b)   a man accursed, devoted to the direst of woes

Part of Speech: noun neuter

A Related Word by Thayer's/Strong's Number: from _G394_

Citing in TDNT: 1:354, 57

A man who is devoted to the direst of woes! What is the direst of woes but the Eternal Fire? In fact some translations of the Bible, translate it as saying, "...let him be eternally condemned."

As the Bible says, if anyone preaches any other Gospel than the one true Gospel, he is condemned to eternal death. We read that a novice in the faith must not become a bishop lest he fall into condemnation. As it is written,

> "not a novice, lest being puffed up with pride he fall into the same condemnation as the devil."   1Ti 3:6

Why would this be? Because he doesn't know the doctrine, yet having pride he claims his words are truth and so sways the faith of many. God is truth and to preach anything other than His one truth is to preach Satan, seeing that Satan is the father of all lies. But that people believe the doctrines of demons is evident. As we read,

> "Now the Spirit expressly says that in latter times some will depart from the faith,

giving heed to deceiving spirits and doctrines
of demons"   1Ti 4:1

Indeed any form of false doctrine is Satan's doctrine.
Can we be saved living out Satan's doctrine? We know that
God has grace but if we refuse to seek the truth then we
aren't serious about our relationship with Jesus. When we
seek the truth we seek Jesus. For Jesus is the truth! As we
read,

> "Jesus said to him, 'I am the way, _the truth_, and
> the life. No one comes to the Father except
> through Me.'"   John 14:6

No one comes to the Father except through the truth,
and that truth is found in Jesus Christ. We know that faith
saves us, but what does faith comes from, the word of Satan
or the word of God?

How then can we be saved if we don't live out the
Gospel? We aren't living it out if we're practicing things
contrary to truth. We can't be saved unless we put our faith
in the exact words of Jesus Christ. But that we aren't saved
unless we continue in truth is evident. For it is written,

> "Brethren, if anyone among you wanders from
> the truth, and someone turns him back, let
> him know that he who turns a sinner from the
> error of his way will save a soul from death and
> cover a multitude of sins."   Jas 5:19-20

The word of God cannot be argued with. It is God spoken and immaculate. As we just read, those who wander from the truth abide in death and are committing a multitude of sins. Jesus is the truth and we must abide in Him. As we discussed in a previous habit,

> "Abide in Me, and I in you. As the branch cannot bear fruit of itself, unless it abides in the vine, neither can you, unless you abide in Me. I am the vine, you are the branches. He who abides in Me, and I in him, bears much fruit; for without Me you can do nothing. If anyone does not abide in Me, he is cast out as a branch and is withered; and they gather them and throw them into the fire, and they are burned."
>
> John 15:4-6

If we do not abide in Jesus, or that is to say 'continue,' we are cast out as a branch and thrown into the fire. What fire do you suppose that is? Obviously the Eternal Fire. Similarly we must continue in the truth. Jesus is the truth and to continue in it is also to continue in Him.

God commands us to be seekers of the truth. Jesus is the truth, and to seek Him is to seek the truth. We need to take these things to heart. This cannot be taken lightly. We must take it with the utmost fear for God and become partakers of the truth. But can we find all truth in this life or is a search for the truth a lifelong process? What do we read?

> "However, when He, the Spirit of truth, has

come, He will guide you into _all_ truth…"

John 16:13

The Holy Spirit guides us into _all_ truth. Not half-truths, not partial truths, but _all_ truth. If then we are led by the Spirit then we will find the truth and come to know it perfectly. God cannot lie. Therefore when He speaks to us through the Holy Spirit, He is leading us in the truth.

Knowing this we must learn to be led by the Spirit in all things. If we learn to be led by Him and to grow in discernment of His voice then we shall find the truth in all things. Also when we read the scriptures the Holy Spirit will read them to us and speak to us through them if we listen for His voice.

It is always good to pray before you read the word and to ask the Lord to read it to you. Ask Him to guide you to where He wants you to read, and ask Him to bring the words to life. Pray that He will breathe life into the pages, and you will begin to hear God like never before. The pages will jump out at you with a newness of life.

When the pages seem to come alive, this is the Holy Spirit talking. Get acquainted with His voice, and learn what it sounds like. Grow in discernment of His voice and God will grow you in the truth.

If you have an issue understanding a doctrine then sit down and seek the Lord in the word. Have a Bible study with Jesus and He will lead you to truth. As you read the word, pray and ask the Lord to guide you through the pages. Pray that He would reveal the truth to you. You know what

His voice sounds like, so don't stop seeking Him until He gives you an answer. It could take a daily study for months to get the answer you're looking for, but if that's the case then at least you're spending that time in the Lord's presence and growing in Him.

Beloved, it's a beautiful thing to spend your whole day seeking Him. It wakes you up in the Spirit and gives you joy daily. If you're going through a hard time, seek Him! His presence will bring you joy and strengthen you in the hardest of times!

I've been through so many trials, and I've learned that the greatest way to get through them is with a smile on your face. And how can you get that smile? By being with Jesus all day. Nothing could make you happier than to spend your day with Him!

I've had many people say to me, "Adam, if I were going through what you were going through I couldn't handle it. I probably would want to take my life! But you just bounce right back from everything. How do you do it?"

Do you see how that can encourage a brother or a sister? Do you see how that gives an awesome witnessing opportunity for an unbeliever? The joy of the Lord in you makes them see the difference between them and God. This difference makes them see their need for Him. When they see the joy and the goodness of Christ in you they are drawn to Him. There is no greater way to lead them to salvation than through being the image of both His love and His joy.

When things get hard, turn to the Lord. And when

you're hurting, run to Jesus. He will hold you in His arms and comfort you until He makes everything better.

When my second son was a two-year-old he was a very top heavy child. His cute oversized toddler head found its way into every hard thing. Then to make matters worse for him, his massive feet would get tangled in just about everything. So needless to say, in his awkwardness he was always getting bumps and bruises.

Many were the times that he tripped and hit his poor little head, then with tears in his eyes he turned and ran to me. I couldn't help but to stretch out my hands and say, "Oh come here my baby, daddy will make it all better!" And I'd hug him, kiss him, snuggle him, and make it all better.

I'm sure that plenty of you parents can relate to this. This is how the Lord looks at us. But if we don't run to Him when we're hurting, it breaks His heart. When we're comforted by Him it grows our relationship with Him. We should seek Him not only in our pleasures but in our pains as well.

How would that make you feel, especially you mothers, if your baby would rather run and cry in a dark corner, than come to mommy for comfort and kisses? Wouldn't your heart just sink?

How do you think that makes the Lord feel when you don't release the issues of your heart to Him? He loves you and wants to cherish you! So let Him!

I would like to encourage you to spend every moment of your days with the Lord, and when things are hard, spend even more time with Him. He will be your strength to overcome every trial that comes your way.

We know that His company will create good morals in us. The more time we spend sitting in His presence the more we will become like Him. Similar to how we read,

> "Do not be deceived: 'Evil company corrupts good habits.'"   1Co 15:33

How much more will the company of God create good habits which lead to life? The more we listen to Him the clearer His voice will become. His voice will be easier to discern and His commands easier to obey. We are saved through faith in His word. So the easier it is to understand Him the better.

We are in the middle of a war with Satan and his angels. Seeing that you are a soldier of God, wouldn't you like to know what God commands you? If we are in the middle of an intense gun fight, would you ignore the Commander's shouts, and do your own thing? Or would you listen to the One who knows what He's doing and how to save your life? While bullets are flying, it would be a bad time to form your own interpretation of His command. You will lose your life.

Even so, this is what is happening to the church _NOW_. We're in the middle of an intense battle with Satan until we go home to the Lord. We _MUST NOT_ interpret our Lord and General's commands. He is the only one who has what it takes to defeat this host of enemies.

But everyone still forms their own opinion! Bullets are

flying and people are jumping up to walk around. We need to take our own walks more seriously than this. We _MUST_ take our relationship more seriously than this.

We must not interpret the Scriptures, but allow the Holy Spirit to explain them to us. We must be more fervent for the truth! We must be more fervent for the Lord!

Look at King Josiah. He was very righteous and poured his whole heart out to obey the Lord and cleanse the land of false doctrine. He had tremendous zeal and a heart of fire. Even his name means, "The fire of the Lord." We need to have hearts more like his!

Although he always had a heart for the Lord when did he become most zealous for Him? When the word of God entered his heart. As we read,

> "Then Shaphan the scribe showed the king, saying, 'Hilkiah the priest has given me a book.' And Shaphan read it before the king. Now it happened, when the king heard the words of the Book of the Law, that he tore his clothes.

> "Then the king commanded Hilkiah the priest, Ahikam the son of Shaphan, Achbor the son of Michaiah, Shaphan the scribe, and Asaiah a servant of the king, saying, 'Go, inquire of the Lord for me, for the people and for all Judah, concerning the words of this book that has

been found; for great is the wrath of the Lord that is aroused against us, because our fathers have not obeyed the words of this book, to do according to all that is written concerning us.'"   2Ki 22:10-13

Up until this time people were not living by the word of God in truth. They sought to please the Lord of their own works. The priests of the temple should have known all about the book! But what did the scriptures say? "We found a book," which suggests that it was previously lost and unaccounted for. Thus people worshipped God in the manner they felt was best. But what do we read in regard to this?

"...For great is the wrath of the Lord that is aroused against us, because our fathers have not obeyed the words of this book, to do according to all that is written concerning us."
                                    2Ki 22:13

The word of God must enter our heart. We must live it out in truth. We must honor the Lord according to His word. After reading the word of God, Josiah was so zealous and convicted that he stood up and forced the nation to make an oath to God. As we read,

"Then the king stood in his place and made a covenant before the Lord, to follow the Lord, and to keep His commandments and His testimonies and His statutes with all his heart and all his soul, to perform the words of the covenant that were written in this book. And he made all who were present in Jerusalem and Benjamin take a stand. So the inhabitants of Jerusalem did according to the covenant of God, the God of their fathers."

2Ch 34:31-32

When we gave our lives to Christ we made an oath with Him to follow Him and obey His commandments and testimonies. How are we fulfilling this covenant by having so many different doctrines? What is truth anymore? It seems that it is merely an opinion, and is no longer our singular and solid foundation. We need truth and we need it now! Never has there been a more dire need for it.

False doctrine is everywhere. It's as plentiful as water, and every drop is poisoned. In every church everywhere one person or another is sharing this poison water with others and bringing people to a dance of death. False doctrine isn't treated the way it should be: as a nasty poison that must be eradicated.

Those of you who are pastors should make your church take a stand for the Lord, and make an agreement before Him to search after truth and true doctrine with all their hearts, souls, minds, and strength. To seek the truth is to seek Jesus and we are commanded to love Him with all our hearts, souls, minds, and strength.

If we obey the commandment to love the Lord our

God, seeing that Jesus is the truth, we will seek truth with all our heart. We must make it our priority and passion to live according to it, and to walk in it daily. In this He will be well pleased in us. As it is written,

> "I have no greater joy than to hear that my children walk in truth." 3Jn 1:4

It is sin to live according to your opinions about Christ. There is only one doctrine, and we are called to seek it and live according to it. But many act as if it's okay to think what you want to and have whatever opinion you want. Our opinions aren't truth, God's word is.

But it's part of the 'new age.' "You do your thing and I'll do mine, I'll accept you the way you are and you accept me the way I am."

That's not what Christ calls us to. He calls us to be unified in the same doctrine. Even as it is written,

> "Now I plead with you, brethren, by the name of our Lord Jesus Christ, that you all speak the same thing, and that there be no divisions among you, but that you be perfectly joined together in the same mind and in the same judgment." 1Co 1:10

We are called to speak the same thing, but no one is and nobody cares. How horrible is that!? This prayer is a wakeup call. A wakeup to seek pure and perfect doctrine in

Jesus Christ. It can be found! The Lord tells us that the Holy Spirit leads us into _ALL_ truth.

But we have contentions among the churches. One church has one set of core beliefs, and the other has a different set of beliefs. Then some of the church goers act as if their own congregation is the best place to be, and if you're from a different church then you're not as much of a Christian as they.

These are the contentions the scriptures are talking about. But God calls us to unity, and Satan is the author of division. Contention is formed by a difference of opinion. What is happening today is the same thing that was happening in the church of Corinth. As the scripture goes on to say,

> "For it has been declared to me concerning you, my brethren, by those of Chloe's household, that there are contentions among you. Now I say this, that each of you says, 'I am of Paul,' or 'I am of Apollos,' or 'I am of Cephas,' or 'I am of Christ.'" 1Co 1:11-12

We are all doing this! "I am of this church" or "I am of that church." We teach with words like, "As so and so who wrote a book once said." Rather than saying, "as it is written in the word of God." Our unity is found in Jesus Christ, not authors or preachers or pastors. Preachers, pastors, and teachers need to be pointing everyone to Jesus, by Whom they can unify the churches. We as teachers need to be living arrows, always pointing the church back to God. All teachings need to be brought back to the word _always_. By His word we are saved and by His word we are unified.

Also we ought to be of the same body, but in different buildings. So what if your church is called "Willow" and their church is "Calvary?" We must act as brothers and family. Too many people act as if their church is the best. What we should be doing is going where God calls us, and treat each other like family. We are a family, a real family, but we're horribly divided.

So God called you to "Willow" and God called them to "Calvary." Does this then make anyone superior than the other? Is one brother better than the other? What did the Lord say to the Apostles when they argued who would be the greatest in heaven? He told them to give glory to God because there is no one greater than the Father. Why then are we stuck on the premise of comparing ourselves and our churches to one another? But as it is written,

> "For we dare not class ourselves or compare
> ourselves with those who commend themselves.
> But they, measuring themselves by themselves,
> and comparing themselves among themselves,
> are not wise."   2Co 10:12

So are you better than the other for going to a certain church? No, but both of you are obedient to God in where you are led and fed. Treat each other with dignity, and save each other from trials. Act as a loving body, although you come from different buildings. Who cares where they go, just love them as God commanded you. Then you will fulfill the commandments. Thus you will be like Josiah in making your oath.

Josiah more or less was telling God, "I don't know if anyone else will obey you and be fervent for you." Then as he raised his hand to God he cried out, "But at least I know there is this one who will be!"

Let us go and do likewise. If no one else will do rightly and seek truth at least you will. Be fervent to love God and each other, and be fervent to know His doctrine. It will save you and all those who hear you. As it is written,

> "Take heed to yourself and to the doctrine. Continue in them, for in doing this you will save both yourself and those who hear you."
>
> 1Ti 4:16

But because we squabble amongst ourselves as to what the truth is and to what the best church is, we are not acting spiritual but fleshly. As the scripture went on to say in Corinthians,

> "For you are still carnal. For where there are envy, strife, and divisions among you, are you not carnal and behaving like mere men? For when one says, 'I am of Paul,' and another, 'I am of Apollos,' are you not carnal? Who then is Paul, and who is Apollos, but ministers

through whom you believed, as the Lord gave
to each one?"   1Co 3:3-5

God gave each teacher and each church to meet the believer where they're at. These are God's chosen instruments and God's chosen tools. But nevertheless God is still the Master Craftsman. Let Him shape your heart. Let Him form His mind in you. Let Him lead you to truth.

Besides if you're the one doing the loving, they will see God in you and more likely be drawn to your church anyway. Yes, one church may have a more solid teaching than the other, due to the pastor's decisions, but having superior wisdom doesn't make us superior people. We *should* be where there is superior wisdom, but without love wisdom means nothing. We are called to humble ourselves and wash each other's feet with the water of the word. Jesus came to serve not to be served. If we love according to truth and lead others to it, they will naturally be drawn to the right church. If you want more people to come to your church, then focus on filling the people and not the pews. Afterward, the people will come naturally, and God will bless it.

At this time I would like to call you to devote yourself to God in seeking pure doctrine. There is only one truth, and it is the only way to salvation. We need to be fervent for it, and fervent to seek it. We need to teach our churches to be fervent for it. We must teach these things to our children, and everyone we disciple.

We must seek perfect and complete truth in Jesus Christ, no matter the cost. This will unify us all, near and abroad. We will come to unity over doctrine just by listening to the Holy Spirit. He leads and guides us all the same way. By seeking Him for truth we will find unity. We will be of the same mind and the same judgment. Take this time to devote yourself to seeking pure and perfect doctrine for the rest of your life.

The Prayer,

"God, I commit myself to You to find Your truth in everything. Lord I fear You and know that those who don't live according Your gospel can't be saved. I love Your truth. I commit my life to seeking Your pure and perfect doctrine. I also commit my life to teach others to do the same."

The Lord's Answer,

"I have no greater joy than to hear that my children walk in truth! You have no idea how much you delighted Me with that prayer! I love you, and it *is* My will for you to have truth. It is My *immediate* will and I will lead you to it, and you shall know it! Only seek it with all your heart and have faith in Me that I can deliver it to you perfectly through My Holy Spirit."

Prayer Five

Walking In Love

WHEN WE GROW in love we also learn to grow in kindness. Love and kindness go hand in hand. To show kindness requires us to see need, and fulfill it. It requires us to be hospitable. Hospitality and kindness give a person a reputation. It's not often that we see someone fully grown in having a servant's heart.

I had a friend many years ago who invited me to his father's house, which was on the other side of the state. We were going to spend the night, and just as we were arriving this man said to me, "I can't wait for you to meet my father's wife; she's so virtuous!" Now this was not his mother but His father was remarried to another woman. I asked him what he meant by virtuous, and he said, "Just wait until you meet her!" That's all he said and he wouldn't tell me an ounce more.

When I arrived at their house, within seconds after meeting her and shaking her hand she immediately helped me out of my coat and pulled up a chair for me. She offered me something to drink, and made sure I was fed. The next morning she woke up very early to set breakfast. We were in a hurry so she lined up boxes of cereal, and a gallon of milk. She had spoons and bowls all washed, ready and waiting for us. As we left for church she helped me with my coat and everyone else's as we left.

Now this may sound like anyone being a good hostess of a guest but she wasn't acting like a hostess. This wasn't an act at all. This was her normal practice every day for everyone she encountered. She never complained about it, but grew to have joy in it. She served everyone happily, especially her husband. She always took her walk with Christ seriously and served her husband constantly. This was such an encouragement to him that he also became a serving giving person.

When I made my way to the living room, he sat me down in his best chair, and said, "Here, put your feet up!" He pulled his lever and kicked me back in style. Then he looked down at my feet and noticed a hole in my sock. So He ran up the stairs without a word. To my dismay this man came waltzing down to me armed with a pair of expensive and very comfortable socks.

"Oh you don't have to do that!" I said.

"Nonsense," he replied as he knelt down and peeled off my socks.

"These are comfortable and you should wear them!"

And he put his own socks on me.

Again, you could think that these people were just trying to be good hosts, but according to their son's testimony it wasn't the case. They were always caring, kind, and giving. Their actions greatly encouraged my friend. He always _LOVED_ visiting his dad. He felt closer to His father through the kindness he saw. It deeply encouraged him and made him want to do the same in his life. His father was able to use kindness to draw his son close to him. Then through his closeness he was able to firmly admonish his son according to his need. And in all of this his son deeply respected him.

Kindness is something we should always be growing in. A little bit of kindness can go a long way. It refreshes a weary soul, and encourages a person to go and do likewise. Kindness sparks a fire in a person's heart. It inspires them to do good and not evil. By showing kindness we can turn others to righteousness. This is exactly what Jesus did. As we hear in the song "kindness" performed by Chris Tomlin: "It's your kindness Lord that leads us to repentance, your favor Lord is our desire." (This is coming from Romans 2:4)

It's the goodness and kindness of Jesus Christ that leads us to salvation. This is because His kindness convicts us. Without kindness we could never be saved. But even as we said before, hospitality and kindness give a person a reputation.

At the time of this writing, I have met thousands of people over the past seven years since that happened. But I only met this couple once and I still remember their kindness after spending only one day with them. I can't even remember their names, but I remember their kindness.

I was very weary at the time, and they refreshed and encouraged me. So much so, that I am still encouraged by them seven years later.

Take the time to grow in loving kindness. Love covers a multitude of sins and kindness leads us to repentance. It can save the unbeliever, and encourage the believer.

The Prayer,

"Lord I commit myself to having a servant's heart. Make my heart like Yours. Please open my eyes to see those in need around me, and give me what is necessary to deliver them. Work in me and through me that You may be glorified. I surrender to Your guiding hand in my life, and devote myself to this forever. Teach me how to love like You. I want to honor You in all things."

The Lord's Answer,

"Love is the substance of who I AM. Without love you can never know Me. I AM love, and because I have loved you, you are saved. Nothing could please Me more than for you to love your brethren. So take care of them and nurture them. Not just the ones you know, but love everyone and tend to their needs.

"Love your enemies. Didn't you see Me pray for My enemies when I was crucified by them? Remember that I was crucified for you while you were yet My enemy. While you still walked in sin I loved you! I loved you but rebuked you that you could repent and become My child. Go and do likewise, and you will find that I am with you. My heart and My hand are yours."

SEASONING OUR WORDS WITH SALT

"LET YOUR SPEECH always be with grace, seasoned with salt, that you may know how you ought to answer each one." Col 4:6

Jesus tells us,

"...For out of the abundance of the heart the mouth speaks. A good man out of the good treasure of his heart brings forth good things, and an evil man out of the evil treasure brings forth evil things. But I say to you that for every idle word men may speak, they will give account of it in the Day of Judgment."

Mat 12:34-36

If we seek to have a pure heart, then we also need to

have pure words. Words that heal, words that bring peace and truth. Words that are devoted to goodness.

When we speak negatively it can discourage, break down, and destroy. But when we choose words that heal, they can edify build up and strengthen.

Be a person dedicated to healing words. Look for those who have downcast souls and life them up in the love of God. Remember that Jesus is a healer and not a destroyer. Sometimes our words can break down and already broken person. There are times that we may speak hurtful words without even realizing it. But if we are loving the other person as we should then we will be attentive to their state of heart and choose words that heal.

Sometimes healing words need to be firmly spoken in love. One such example would be when a brother or sister is caught in a pattern of sin. Some people don't lovingly rebuke as they should. "Well, I don't want to be one who judges," some may say. But we aren't judging these situation, merely discerning. Also, we aren't condemning, but turning to the Lord for spiritual healing.

Loving discernment would be one that points a brother or sister to the Lord. If they aren't honoring the Lord, nothing could be more loving than to come behind them and encourage them to do rightly. Yet in a few cases some people may need a truly firm rebuke.

For those few who fall wildly in love with their sin, having known better, they need firmer admonishment. Also for anyone who is insubordinate to the Lord, and refusing to do rightly after being rebuked, they may need some firmness. As we read,

> "For there are many insubordinate, both idle talkers and deceivers, especially those of the circumcision, whose mouths must be stopped, who subvert whole households, teaching things which they ought not, for the sake of dishonest gain. One of them, a prophet of their own, said, "Cretans are always liars, evil beasts, lazy gluttons." This testimony is true. _Therefore rebuke them sharply, that they may be sound in the faith_"
> Titus 1:10-13

Such a person knows the truth, but seeks to benefit only their flesh. They remain insubordinate to the Holy Spirit and thus must be rebuked sharply, yet in all wisdom and with all love. God will give you discernment as to how you should approach anyone's situation. Remain attentive to the Holy Spirit, and always be looking for opportunities for words that heal, and draw others near to Christ.

Sometimes struggling with kind or healing words toward others isn't the only issue. There are times that in brokenness and self-defeat we speak poorly of ourselves. When we allow our souls to be "down cast" (as David put it) we create more harm than good.

For example, when we sin we start to beat ourselves up over our failures. God doesn't call us to negative self-speech, but to glorify Him. In repentance God has grace. When we make the decision to do rightly, it's time to lift up our heads and glorify the Lord. When we look down at ourselves, we aren't looking up at the goodness of God.

A discouraged heart can lead to a downcast soul. A downcast soul can lead to self-condemnation and negative self-speech. If we want our words to be seasoned with salt then we need to turn our tears of defeat into songs of praise because of God's triumph. He has overcome our sin, and overwhelmed us in forgiveness and love.

When we can't get it right, it's because we've been approaching victory incorrectly –whether in sin or in other issues of life. We have to remember that it's God who works in us for victory. When we submit to our flesh, or work things out in our own strength, we fail. But when we lean on Christ we find the strength to stand. By remembering these things, we find good reason to lift up our heads in praise.

If we are giving glory to the Lord in everything we say, our speech will reflect it. Our tongues should always be seasoned with salt. Sometimes it's good to ask ourselves before we talk, "Is this going to glorify the Lord, and turn this person to Jesus?" If not then we shouldn't be saying it.

Negative speech toward others can be damaging. Hurtful speech is easy to categorize as harmful. But sometimes we overlook the importance of abstaining from coarse joking, and idle speech.

Even Jesus said,

> "But I say to you that for every idle word men may speak, they will give account of it in the Day of Judgment. For by your words you will be justified, and by your words you will be condemned."   Mat 12:36-37

Knowing then that we can be condemned for our speech this should lead us to fear. But anyone who pursues a righteous walk will also pursue holy speech which edifies not only themselves but others. If we love one another we will want to edify one another.

The hardest time to say something that turns another back to the Lord is during an argument. We get heated and easily tempted to say something we don't mean. Perhaps in our anger for the moment we mean what we say. But when we start thinking more rationally, we realize that's not our heart at all. So we end up regretting our words.

In this example we see that the words start with the heart. We need to learn to back down and cool off a minute. If we aren't meditating on the Lord, in our anger we will let something slip. It's good to remember to cool off and spend some time with God. Think about the situation, then go back and speak when your heart is sober.

In the drunkenness of anger we speak like fools. By learning to temper our hearts and curb our anger, proper convicting words will come out instead. In this we can lead one another to Christ, and thus we can find peace and unity through Him.

But we also need to remember to recognize when others

are struggling. If they need to sit back, cool off, and be with God, then we need to stop pressing our side of the argument. Let them return to a proper and sober mind in Christ. If you push them, they'll explode. It's like squeezing a balloon filled with rotten milk to the point of bursting. On whom will the milk spill? If then you want the pure milk of God from their mouth, encourage them to spend some time with God, and agree together that you both need to cool off. Agree to come back immediately afterward and work out the issue.

We need to temper our hearts to be holy and loving in everything. Satan loves to seize the moments of our wrath and bring in further division. Lost friendships and broken relationships are not worth the few costly words we speak. If we change our hearts and lips, those relationships would be built up rather than broken down.

Learning to back down and be meek is vital. If you or the other person are too angry or disagreeable then you need to have a few moments with the Lord. Blow off some steam to God, pray with an upright heart. Ask the Lord Who sees everything, "Am I wrong in anything?" Then have an open heart to hear from Him. Time and time again, there was always a little something God pointed out that I didn't realize I was doing. Then I would go and immediately apologize.

Seeking unity needs to be the priority when arguing, not expressing opinions. If we have a heart to seek unity we will find it. Even Jesus said, "Seek and you shall find."

Sometimes it's good to say sorry right away. Even if you feel only a little wrong, say sorry right away. It will break the tension and bring everyone back to a sober mind. Then after you think about it, you may realize that you were more than a little wrong. By saying sorry you avoided a bad fight turning into a worse one.

Don't worry about what the other person is doing, always be the first to bring unity. Let the responsibility begin with us as we seek to grow in the Lord and please Him. If our hearts are right before God, our words will be right.

Ultimately, whether in arguments or in unholy speech, seeking mouths of grace must be our priority. By words we can build up and draw near to Christ, and by words we can break down and turn one away from the Lord. Like an industrial wrecking ball through a house, our words can ruin a home.

Take this time to devote yourself to wholesome speech. Words that turn others to Jesus. Seek sound godly speech which cannot be condemned. As it is written,

> "in all things showing yourself to be a pattern of good works; in doctrine showing integrity, reverence, incorruptibility, sound speech that cannot be condemned, that one who is an opponent may be ashamed, having nothing evil to say of you."   Tit 2:7-8

Ultimately Jesus said that our words come from our

heart. If we have sound speech our heart will be well trained as well. Even as we read,

> "A good man out of the good treasure of his heart brings forth good; and an evil man out of the evil treasure of his heart brings forth evil. For out of the abundance of the heart his mouth speaks." Luk 6:45

And also,

> "For we all stumble in many things. If anyone does not stumble in word, he is a perfect man, able also to bridle the whole body." Jas 3:2

Knowing this we should make our aim to have holy mouths with everything we say. Let's dedicate ourselves to building one another up. Let's have holy words that edify and heal. By changing our words it will change our hearts. By changing our hearts and the way we act in and respond to life it will change our lives forever.

The Prayer,

"Lord I dedicate myself from this time forward to having words that edify and heal. I know Your judgment and fear You. Bring holiness to my mouth. Give me words that heal, and bring peace. Be my strength in my weaknesses as I commit myself to You."

The Lord's Answer,

"Beloved, every word of Mine is Holy. My words always lead you back to Me. They bring salvation and life. Therefore My words never return to Me void.

"Let not your words return to you void. Let them produce life in others, as I have produced life in you. I will judge you according to your words, and if you brought healing and life, how can I not bless you?

"Grow in Me, and turn others to Me with the things that come from your mouth. Listen to My conviction. My Spirit will be with you and teach you the things you should say and do."

CONTINUAL DEVOTION

OUR DAY TO day activities can be overwhelming. They can distract us from the Lord and tear us down. It is vital for us to give our days to Him. Every morning, every day and every evening needs to be the Lord's. When our days wear us down, God will breathe new life in us.

But spending the day with Him doesn't negate the need for a genuine time of devotion. We need to remember to take the time to set aside all distractions and find God in the secret place. The secret place is where we find our greatest renewal and growth. God communicates His heart to us, and refreshes us in His Spirit. As we sit on Daddy's lap, He reads His word to us, and explains its meaning to us. If you've been worn out by the stresses of life, remember to spend time in devotion to the Lord every day.

Be rejuvenated by His Spirit and strengthened by His presence. If you've been occupied with the busy-ness of life, take this time to rededicate yourself to daily devotion.

Remember to be strengthened by Him and be edified by His presence.

The Prayer,

"Lord strengthen me through my day. Give me strength to sit daily in Your presence. From this point forward I will continue in a daily devotion, spending time with You alone, every day."

The Lord's Answer,

"I can't wait! Will you spend a little time with Me tonight? I want to be with you! You're so precious to Me!

"Come away from the world around you. Even if for a little bit, and spend some time with Me. It would mean so much to Me, and it will strengthen you.

"I will refresh and rejuvenate you. I will bless you in the abundance of My peace. Beloved, come and find rest in My arms, tonight."